<u>Atychiphobia</u>

By N.P.M.

Preface

I am a scared little child,
Fear gave me structure,
Repetition gave me discipline,
Pain gave me inspiration,

What's a scared child to do,
When they are no longer afraid,
When the repetition stops,
When the pain dulls,

I was a scared little child,
What to thank for my structure,
What to thank for my discipline,
What to thank for my inspiration,

Freedom never scared me,
Freedom from all that hurt me,
The true irony of this book,
The title is my declaration,

I am free.

Crusade for Thy Narcissism

It's me,
That's what matters,
The horrors of greatness,
The cost of failure,

It's me,
That's what matters,
The truest suffering,
The empty curses,

It's me,
That's what matters,
The struggles of addiction,
The oldest religion,

It's me,
That's what matters,
The demons and their corpses,
My holy army,

It's me,
That's what matters,
The day sinking slow,
The night rising fast,

It's me,
That's what matters,
The quickening pace of an irregular heartbeat,
The tightening of it's firm hold,

It's me,
That's what matters,
The I don't know hymns,
I don't owe him,

It's me,
That's what matters,
The gaseous pure omnipotence,
The noxious true omniscience,

It's me,
That's what matters,
The most crucial crusade,
The gates guarded by a saint,

It's me,
That's what matters,
Storming in full force,
Battalion battling for redemption,

Hollow be thy name,
True be thy holy blade,
Cut down by forces rotted and ragged,
Truest wounds on thy wings,
The magnitude of gore sings,
Songs played only by militant bards,
Dragged shall thy body be,
Thousands and thousands of yards,
The battle hardly won,
The army hardly one,
A mountain of corpses by thy sons,
Burning in the sun thy sons,
To who they preyed,
Heathen Speak,
It's Me,
That's What Matters,

UH? VOID

Guaranteed failure is an impossible Twin,
Brought forth by a penal Womb,
Baron are the ovaries of Inability,
Enable nothing in the Void,

Stop,
Stop,
Stop,
Repeat,
Enable nothing the Void;

The void stays still in this Current,
All are one with the Void,
We suffer Together,
An existential pact to make no Impact,
Broken people aren't able to do the Breaking,

We're shaking and we're Itching,
Screaming and Scratching,
Mercy kill or release Us,
Stop Stop Repeat,
Enable nothing in the Void;

No we can speak and Repeat,
Stop the paradox to which we Flock,
with no where else to go,
We are what the void Rot,

Stop,
Repeat,
Stop,
Repeat,
Mercy kill or release Us,
Guaranteed failure maybe an impossible Twin,
brought forth by the cerebellum's womb,
in?
able? nothing in this void;

A Day-A Month-A Year From Now

I address this mess to my future self,
Made the best of nothing I see,
I see you never gave up on me,
I understand you want what you can't have still,

You didn't give into that crippling lack of will,
The voices telling you what to do,
Did you ever listen,
The regrets that you hold,
Do they pump your pistons,
Does your pain power you,

After the world violently deflowered you,
Is all your work swarmed by cliches,
Does your past make you twist and turn,
Do you hate me,
The past you,

So I guess I'm asking,
Do you hate you,
I ask myself if I hate you,
That's because I don't know you,
Yet I know you're better than me,
More evolved than me,

I already resent myself,
Should I resent you too,
These cramps in my hands,
Do they also plague you,
I'm only asking questions,
Are you self centered too?

Shower Song

The water hits me,
Wet hot water down to the knee,
Why is the shower,
Where my brain reminds me to cower,
In disrespectful fashion,
I break away that need to ration,

Only me and my past,
Flying by super fast,
Moment after moment,
No Nerve not spent,
All in the mind,
Remind me that I'm crazy,
Would you be so kind,
Deeper into my complexity,

I'm forcibly spitting out my feelings with simplicity,
All my life,
I've been haunted by this knife,
Cutting deep to create invisible strife,
I know pain,
But that's how I confess,
In my stockholm,
In the blue,
I'm truly,
Obsessed with you.

Ghost

These restrictions,
These Binds,
They Choke me,
You tighten them,
Ever and forever,
I won't be released,
Til my mind ceases,
To want you,

I see fatal beauty,
Fatal cause you hurt,
You bring the pain,
Rocking a man,
Back to the cradle of insanity,
It's no obsession,
Just the most profound want,

I annoy you,
I bug you,
You're the ghost,
Ever haunting my mental,
Let me repeat,
The ghost ever haunting,
Goddamn confidence flaunting,
That beauty increasing my wanting,

This craving,
The barriers I must hop,
To make this stop,
Why can't you,
Make this easier for me,
Why can't I haunt you,
I want to be a ghost too.

Perspective

I'm depressed,
My pain has made my feelings repressed,
The Murphy name is a curse to me,
The things I'm privileged enough to see in me,
The Murphy name will destroy me,

I've destroyed me myself and I,
I've never known what's truly mine,
As every night I sleep,
On a bed of mines,
The Murphy name is mines,

I can't even set the lines,
I cross too damn fast,
I destroy myself me and I,
The only thing I know isn't a lie,
And even when I,
Wants to die,
I cannot cry,
The damn tears,
Dry too fast,

At last I knows,
The Murphy name is a curse to I me and myself,
Shelf myself and it's he him,
Slim chance he likes seeing him,
He strives to not be him,
He hates that he is he,

Murphy has no law,
Him is flawed,
Him only wants to escape he,
He only wants to escape me,
Out of me him and he,
He's the third person to see the wrong in me.

Reminiscence

Traumatic times breed black heirs,
Troubled tantrums spilling out a fountain of despair,
Who's there,
In the darkest times,
The shade is where we all reside,

Hidden under cloaks of repression,
Breeding the killers in us,
Looking for a ticket to confession,
Demonic deities all need disciples,
Ladies and gentlemen grab your rifles,
What's the matter,
Sharing a bed with your own brain splatter,
Hopefully now you can ignore the chatter,
Pitter patter and clatter,
Rhyming verses to distract from morgue hearses,
We all use entertainment,
To forget our curses,
Blinding us to old remedies,
They worked when we were kids,
Now deep dives into the pineal gland,
Turn up nothin,

Bred black heirs lost in the fountain,
They're dread in the water,
Drowning in the sea of memories so abrasive,
Dead and floating because nostalgia,
Is so persuasive!

My Fair Ferryman

My Fair Ferryman,
Carry us upstream!
The fare was Fair-
So fair it was hard to believe!

Against the current we-
Rowed we Rowed we-
Rowed this effort for my money,
Is truly hard to believe,

Then the boat won't go,
The river heartily said no!
A the end of the voyage,
I'm back at the bottom of the stream.

Read Me: Backwards and Forwards

If IQ test were fact over fiction,
I would be a god,
At least I'd be fair,
To the men who despair,
Tearing away at their hair,
So much knowledge to share,
I'd bless the lesser beings,
With ferocious mental and physical beatings,
I'd save the masses from their feelings,
Save them from their limited understandings,
I'll save them from the truly cruel beatings,
Those pathetic human hearts.

Anthem Black

We will never make it,
We are oppressed,
We will never make it,
We are doomed,
We will never make it,
I made it.

Don't cry, you didn't sow in ash.

Father to son,
Son to father,
Not every son,
But every father,
Was a son,
What's a father,
To a son,
A proper cycle,
Not every father,
Was really a sun,
The family nights,
Tend to be alaskan,
Everything slows,
When there's no fun,
When there's no sun,
To a son,
To a father,
Everything is illuminated,
Even without fun,
Sons are fast,
In good soil,
They grow so fast,
To a father,
If he grows,
When he grows,
I hope he grows,
You reap what you sow,
Or the world will reap,
You sowed they reaped,
Sow in ash,
You'll reap ash,
If he grows.

ADULT SWIM

I'm bolting to the door,
I want it more and more,
It's on the bright bold horizon,
I'm getting there so fast,
I never wanted for my childhood to last.

Until it was over,
And the door becomes the shore of a vengeful ocean,
Everything in the back of my mind,
All this time,
Then I realize childhood was sublime.

I see my christmas photos from years ago,
Numerically so close yet I've gone so far,
I sit on the shore without even a toe in the water,
As to not be dragged away,
On land just a look-alike stranger.

The sensation feels like danger,
When they speak,
Through the crashing of the waves on the shores,
The thunder from the ocean storm,
I speak,
You hear my voice and it says goodbye,
You feel appalled by this lie,
You're not going anywhere,
You think,
You thought,
And thought wrong you did,
Because at the blink of an eye you realize,
When bolting for the door you tripped,
Or slipped and fell into the ocean,
Now you're stranded out in sea drowning,
And the water rises,
In our lungs,
The water settles and you settle at the bottom of the ocean,
So we give up on motion,
It's over.

The Slave Narrative Report

Formality whipped my English class,
Formality lynched my English class,
The spirituals are sung,
The Klan robes hung,

Reality was the E.M.T.,
And his aid everyday speak,
To carry my English class away,
The Doctor named Modern Day,
Assisted by Nurse Issues,

In the hospital for discussion,
Turns out my English class,
Just had a concussion.

Bruce Wayne and Other Stupid Masks

Found my super villain,
Never been happier,
Found my nemesis,
Never been happier,
Found my dragon to slay,

That devil to my god,
That beast of Nazareth,
I see you plotting now,

I smell your sulfur scent,
I hear your deep raspy growl,
I taste your rotten flesh,

I know you motherfucker,
There are no windup penguins,
No fucking riddles to solve,
I don't see a killer crocodile,
Just you,
Everyday in the mirror,
Right behind everything I've written,
To feel like the hero.

RAGE

Let it go,
In the reserves,
Let it go,
Fully stocked,
Let it go,
Let it go,
On every repetition,
Grip it tighter,
Hold it tight,
Let it go,
Keep it close,
Never let it go,
That's gasoline,

That's that focus,
That's that pressure,
Never let it go,
Fuel never-ending,
Now see everything,
I see you motherfucker,
I'll grip it like a steering wheel,
Drive myself off the deep end!

BL\EE/D

Viciously rip him apart,
Watch the organs,
The pulsating pink,
Stomach and chest,
Tear into him and give me the rest,
There will be no rest,

Need his teeth,
Drag a hammer across the ivory xylophone,
Watch just the tips melt,
Reveal the white,
Show the red,
No red,

No red but he's dead,
No red in this dead,
He doesn't bleed,
Never noticed,
Caught up in the fun,
Never noticed until the deed was done.

Phantasmagoria: Guilt Personified In The Final Act

Disturb me,
Lose me,
Hate me,
Take me,
Choke me,
Cut me,
Forget me,
Eleanor Louis Cowell;

Disturb me,
Hurt me,
Break me,
Slice me,
Dice me,
Strangle me,
Torture me,
Bind me,
Dorothea Mae Rader;

Disturb me,
Find me,
Grab me,
Quiet me,
Bash me,
Silence me,
Rape me,
Eat me,
Ellen Fish;

Kidnap the women,
Castrate the men,
Smother the infants,
Sodomize the innocent,
Gun down the heroes,
Cut up the pigs,
Butcher the town,
Tie up the families and burn it all down,
Disturb me.

pretty KNUCKLES

HEXAGONS AND RHOMBI,
OH BABY THEY FLY,
NICE AND DRY,
SCRATCHED SCRUNCHED CRACKED AND BRUISED,

why don't they bleed the same,
must be the stronger company replacement,
must be that much more expensive,

UGLY AND MOTLEY,
HARD LIKE CEMENT IN MIDLIFE,
CRISIS AND CRIME,
CAR POOL IN TUNNEL,

who did this to them,
look they're broken again,
kids appreciate nothing,

RUINED AND IMMORTAL,
NEVER COMING BACK NO,
AUTHOR AND PUNISHER,
GOODBYE MY PRETTY KNUCKLES,

they remind in the times of peace,
there is no peace for the depraved,
never forgive such a wasteful child.

Black Eyes

The ringed city of the damned,
Souls lost and abandoned,
Are the less fortunate melodramatic when gored,

Echoing lament bouncing in entrapment,
Their moral ambiguity keeps them chained,
Free to move in chains,

The city chapel walls only come in red,
The night sky only comes in red,
The homes painted in more and more layers of red,

In the dark the damned watch pulsating stars,
The stars beat and rock,
On an axis shaking and another rotating,

Hidden is the ringed city of the damned,
Veiled by black to mortal eyes,
The mortal world with two lone windows,

The foolish living peek inside,
What do they see,
The black veil irritated by proximity,

It claws at the foolish,
Closer,
They just get closer,
Closer,
And closer,
Fools are the ignorant and curious,
Mortals all too adventurous,
Savior has arrived in the form of the veil,
Mortals no longer,
Damned be those who enter the ringed city;

Love

Is it a war of attrition,
Or is it a gift to the gifted,
The better us in mind has shifted,
Fall for a parlor trick and pick up this addiction.

Closet Closest

My dreams never look the same,
The wispy world on monday,
The jagged edges and sharpness of tuesday,
The dreary dystopia on wednesday,

My mondays are ends to my last beginnings,
The tuesday tedium gets to me,
When wednesday just reminds me it's not friday,
Those nights with my closet door open,

My dreams never sound the same,
The tearing and growls of thursday,
The lamentation of wandering souls on friday,
The cheers and uproar of saturday,

Taxing thursday anxiety,
Frozen on friday with my train of thought,
See saturday's demons approach,
Those nights with my closet door open,

Sunday is ironic,
No sun in my room,
My closet is dark,
My closest closet is dark,

I remember as a kid,
My closest closet was dark,
At night I never dreamt,
Is a nightmare a dream,
no.

Once I was no longer a necessity

Words you spoke to me,
They didn't sound the same no,
Not a single word,

They rung in my ear,
Alert Alert Alert oh,
Not a single word,

I feel the sirens,
That invisible impact,
From such few words damn,

Not a single word,
You just spoke so damn gently,
Not so gentle words,

Not a single word,
Each one eviscerating,
Not one missing me,

You spoke oh so gently damn,
That invisible impact,
Each one eviscerating,
Alert Alert Alert oh,
They don't sound the same to me.

Page 28

Here I declare,
The impoverished minds of youth,
Hold no authority,
Over the pre-established social contract,

The perceived deviance,
In my own socialization,
Faulty in their abridged contract,
Holds no authority over me,

The peonic foundation,
In which these schemas are formed,
Shows the true deviance,
Always lied in your third world,

I'm saying,
The uneducated children,
Can tell me nothing,
About what's right or wrong,

What you see as wrong,
The way I grew up,
I only see a twisted sense of right,
Can't tell me nothin.

Damage

In the night's weary grip,
Oh so monstrous things,
Wish to slip away,
Those shallow breaths reminding,

There are tides to pay,
If only it would go,
The greatest misfortune,
There's no other way,

The rising mass,
Cold and musty,
Saline scent surrounded,
Three foot daggers upon its fingertips,

The bipedal beast,
Previously among the drowned,
Long ago crowned,
King of the primordial sea,

Twitching and shaking,
Uncontrollable deeply embedded rage,
Why why why,
Why why,
Why,
Can a beast simulate insanity?

Denial

FUCK-FUCK-FUCK-FUCK-FUCK-FUCK-FUCK-FUCK-FUCK-FUCK-FUCK-FUCK-FUCK,
FUCK-FUCK-FUCK-FUCK-FUCK-FUCK-FUCK-FUCK-FUCK-FUCK-FUCK-FUCK-FUCK,
FUCK-FUCK-FUCK-FUCK-FUCK-FUCK-FUCK-FUCK-FUCK-FUCK-FUCK-FUCK-FUCK,
I guess saying fuck fixed all my problems,
Not that I was mindful enough to solve them,
And everything slowly falls apart,
Then comes burning eyes,
It truly hurt to realize;

I never had writer's block,
The greatest sacrifice isn't what you love,
It's the ability to accept your love was built on a foundation of lies,
In your eyes are the truth,
Swallowed sorrow and previously petty pain,
Now it rains and it won't end until tomorrow,
Why;

I laid up content in our bed of lies,
I was too content to vocalize,
Comfort was never love,
Love is just comfortable,
I was never in love,
I just loved to think I was,
Fuck;

Who am I to dispel my lies,
Who am I to kill the vibe,
Who am I to me,
Who even was I supposed to be,
I never earned the right to see;

Demolition

I blew up just to blow up,
The words of a dead celebrity,
I blew up just to blow up,
Acknowledging the double speak,

I lit my fuse,
As if my own ruse,
Was passionately abused,
I blew up just to blow up,

Acknowledging the double speak,
As if Im supposed to lick my wounds,
I lit my fuse,
I blew up just to blow up,

My ego so expertly bruised,
As if passionately abused,
The ruse is up,
I blew up just to blow up,

I blew up over you,
On a count of two,
I ran arms wide head high too,
Once safely in my embrace,
There's a change in the look of my face,
You feel the vest,
Wasn't alive long enough to realize the rest,
I blew up over you,
I lit my fuse,
Acknowledging the double speak,
Their egos are so viciously abused bruised and used,
The ruse is truly up,
The time is up,
I'm in pieces because I blew up just to blow up.

FUCK HIGHSCHOOL: A letter to all the nine to five teachers

I'm so sick and tired,
Of this bullshit,
It doesn't feel worth it,
My brain is already retired,

The curriculum that fosters,
The mockery of me,
I haven't learned shit,
Do I look like an idiot,

I've had amazing teachers,
This ain't it,
Why did I have more rigor,
In the goddamn eighth grade,

Calling a spade a spade,
This isn't education,
Wasting my time fueling my frustration,
Bringing me to the revelation,

Speak and repeat,
Not education,
Hand holding and condensation,
Not education,
Sheet after sheet,
Not education,
Let the videos teach,
Not education,
No repetition and motivation,
Not education,
You rarely actually teach,
And we wonder why our children,
Learn more on a sunday listening to Dan Carlin,

And why students want to sleep,
And why students don't want to reach,
And why students give up,
We're all fed up,
Swallow your opinion and teach,
We're not paid to learn,
If you think for a second,
It's a fucking reach,
To think there's a better way to teach,
Don't fucking teach,
Knowledge could be a satisfying payment,
If only you'd connect with me,
Please god don't fucking teach,
Call a replacement,
If you aren't passionate enough to connect with me,
That effort shines like the north star over the dark arctic sea,
But so many don't even care to pretend to be,
Genuinely invested in me,
And me,
And me,
And me,
Hundreds over and over,
Begging desperately,
Connect with me,
Or don't fucking teach.

The Comedian

I'm going crazy,
Baby I think I'm going crazy,
I can't think,
Sentences are hard,
Save me,

I'm depressed,
I need rest,
And more rest,
My feelings so deeply repressed,

I can't focus anymore,
I feel dizzy,
Baby I'm fucking crazy,
So few options to explore,

They keep screaming for more,
I don't wanna be on stage anymore,
But I can't find the fucking door,
Save me before they learn more,

Please explain to me,
Why they're all laughing at me,
I didn't know I was a goddamn comedy,

I don't see anything fucking funny,
Baby please save me,
Baby please save me,
I don't see anything fucking funny,

I don't want their tainted money,
I don't need their toxic company,
I don't feel they truly love me,
I don't get why they must break me.

Oreo Cookie love

I hope my filling was filling,
Careful not to leave it on your lips,
Not the only sugar you got,
I hope I was sweet enough.

I talk a lot, but not always I promise

Little nigga close your mouth,
Please shut the fuck up,
Do you ever stop talking,
I guess yeah when it's dark,

I like the sound of my voice like an old friend,
Comfort in familiar tones,
My inhibitions just skip my mouth,
I'm sorry,

I don't mean to talk so much,
Just spent a lot of time alone,
I've spent a lot of time being unheard,
Even more time finding the right word,

I don't know if there's a lotta noise around me,
Too much noise inside my head,
And a whole lotta bangs and bumps,
Focus has the same old humps,

I can't think no matter how hard I try,
It's all scrambled and jumbled,
So the chaos gets to me,
And I'll feel the need to speak,

Please shut the fuck up,
I'll say it if you won't,
Please shut fuck up,
I'll say it if you won't,

I ask myself everyday all day,
To be quiet,
Look around and create an environment,
Without a sound,

But even in the most peaceful quiet,
There's screaming inside my head,
I twitch when I lay in bed,
And the screaming never stops;

Training Day

Imma spit rhymes never heard before,
Shit so sick turn niggas into herbivores,
Gang Bangers Slip Deep and Preach ridin to the liquor store,
Twelve sleep so they plannin to act out,
Three dip out their white subaru to do evil,
They reach up to grip fabric and get medieval;

Setting,
Little liquor store off elm street,
Time,
Two in the morning,
Characters,
Three loaded Glock Forty-Fives and a kitchen knife,
Props,
Three goons in masks,

Cashier half asleep,
Who's near,
Slip Deep and Preach,
The Cashier nearly falls off his seat,
Before seeing Preach reach and hearing him screech,
Namesake staked on the money he make,
Ironic names irritate primates and third rates,
At a third of the normal rate The Cashier sees,
A helping hand to help him sleep;

Enough force will make a brain cell hesitate,
Wait for the blood to gush down his face,
Race to the floor yes between his body and his blood,
Floods his lungs while his body thuds,
Slip and Preach wanna smoke break,
Make this nigga wake up and stay up and stay tough,
Enough time to use this man's face as a scrub,
Rub it up down leave no blood on the ground,
Sounds remind Deep of the mounds they built,
Guilt riddled he thinks of the rounds they spilt,
Behind Deep of course they're kicking the corpse,
This sadistic shit may not sound realistic but these demons exist;

Deep was never bright but his bulb lights,
Deep feeling bold on this night grips his gun,
Deep is done he lifts it and interrupts Slip and Preach's fun,
Deep covers Preach in Slip's thought's like he asked what's the matter,
Deep blast Slip above the lip before he's used to the splatter,
Deep drops to the ground without a sound to be heard,
Deep's mind is succumbing to the chaos in his own quiet words,
Deep's suppression of his humanity for vanity is eating his sanity,
Deep wishes he'd seen what he'd be in a future nobody should even see,
Deep at one point had passion and goals he wanted to meet,
Deep was young when he fell so he turned to the streets,
Deep had spent too much time seeing his mom savagely beat,
Deep decided to join a new family for some form of safety,
Deep's Pops popped up chopped up all over the place;

Sorrow in his face,
Breathing slows in pace,
No way to escape without a trace,
Regret burning in his eyes like mace,
Traded chance to live with grace,
Until it was hell bound his soul was a hollow base,
At fourteen he's gonna die in this newly forsaken place,
He'll never get to make his case,
As if he would,
If he could,
Cause on his last day,
The last words he'll ever say,
Was the promise he gave his mom today,
Before he went out with his gang to play,
The money will help us get far away,
Ringing in his head before his thoughts coated the store shelves.

Forgot about Rodney

March for them,
Feel the love,
That desired warmth,
We walk together;

We talk as one,
Take our stride with pride,
Monolithic mass on blast,
I'm not doing this;

Beat these niggers,
Batter em blacker,
Beat em ragged,
Blast em down to ash;

These weren't criminals,
Hunted by blue suit punishers,
Why we march together,
Only in good weather;

Our spirits can't be weathered,
Uncontested in protest,
We profess true disapproval,
Vocal enough to completely forget;

Let the dog bites,
Tuck em in tonight,
Broken bones comfort wicked hearts,
While we watch them get torn apart;

We fight for modern diversity,
We fight for equality,
We fight for the disenfranchised,
Get Out;

Watch a real black out,
When the blacks out,

Covering the streets,
Spread of bodies and teeth;

Oh now we ain't civil about civil rights,
Oh now we're angry,
Oh now we're taking a stand,
Get Out;

Three fifths of my brother left,
Left to fend for black lives,
Over jokes and movies,
Gaslighting the gassed up;

Today we march for the remembered,
Seems we've forgotten,
Look backwards and be reminded,
The black way to dress and impress,
Red on my Jays,
Black on my face,
Space in my teeth,
My eye rollin on the road,
When I'm beaten in the street;

I hate you niggas,
I hate you niggers,
I hate you with heart,
I'll tear you apart,
What the fuck were you doin,
Solvin problems bred from sensitivity,
No humility for the past warriors,
Put up the fist,
Motherfucker you took zero risks,
Put up the fist,
As you cower;

If I see one more bystander,
Stand by as I hit the guillotine,
Only woke for seven seconds,
As a severed head,
Oh you did so much to shield me,
Oh you did so much to help me,
I am gracious,
The gratitude of a dead man,

Carry movements into riots,
Activism so effective,
Impoverished minds buy it;

Care so much who's black in fiction,
Brown and white noses like a cocaine addiction,
Understand my diction,
How are you woke,
When so many dead sleep,
I'm starting to see bodies in feeds,
I can't believe,
You already forgot about Rodney;

Snap'd

Honesty Honestly doesn't mean anything,
When you have nothing,
But having nothing is my only honesty,
Isn't that technically something;

Her Last Words

It's ok,
It's over,
Nothing can hurt me anymore,
Don't cry;

It's ok,
It's over,
Nothing can hurt me anymore,
Don't cry;

It's ok,
It's over,
Nothing can hurt me anymore,
Don't cry;

Don't cry Amani,
Don't cry,
Please don't cry Amani,
Don't cry;

But I can't keep a promise,
I cried'
And I cried,
And I cried;

Dracula: Power Personified

Chosen one speak to me,
You must wake the beast,
Slay them my lord,
Show them your sword;

They'll feast their eye,
While you feast on them alive,
They'll taste the metal of your blade,
You'll taste the metal of their veins;

Entrance them all,
It'll be their downfall,
The demons call,
The demons call;

They'll feast their eyes,
As you rise,
From hell to capitalize,
Rise from their blood and lies,

The demons call,
Humor them all,
The Demon's call,
Feed on them all;

Prince of darkness,
We worship,
Death,
We worship,
You.

Sinking

Crash course on the irrational and emotional,
Cut down I am rotted and ragged,
And being depressed makes me pressed,
So Save me Baby please save me,
Don't cry,
You were sweet enough;

Why don't I ever stop talking,
Look I'm broken again,
The greatest misfortune,
My life is a war of attrition,
I have to let it go;

Broken bones comfort my wicked heart,
Yet that invisible impact,
Shows I haven't learned shit,
I blew up just to blow up,
Emotions hold all authority over me;

I'm a fool ignorant and curious,
And my mind has become a vengeful ocean,
I will never make it,
Because my guilt has sought to disturb me,
I'm screaming and scratching the black veil over my psyche;

Until I eventually give up on motion,
Enable nothing I am void,
Of love,
I guess saying fuck fixed all my problems,
Not that I was mindful enough to solve them;

Dedicated to the afraid attempting to be free

Printed in Great Britain
by Amazon